Count Up and Down

By Amanda Gebhardt

2 Miss Dawn's class will count up.

They will start at one.

4 One, two, three ...

Four, five, six ...

Seven, eight, nine, ten.

Miss Dawn is proud!
Her class can count up to ten.

8 Now, the class will count down.

They will start at ten.

Ten, nine, eight ...

Seven, six, five ...

Four, three, two, one.

Miss Dawn claps for her class!

Word List

math words

count	nine	three
down	one	two
eight	seven	up
five	six	
four	ten	

sight words

one

the

to

two

diphthongs

/aw/aw
Dawn

/ow/ou, ow
count

down

proud

Try It!

How fast can you count up to ten
and then back down to one?

Miss Dawn's class will count up.

They will start at one.

One, two, three ...

Four, five, six ...

Seven, eight, nine, ten.

Miss Dawn is proud!

Her class can count up to ten.

Now, the class will count down.

They will start at ten.

Ten, nine, eight ...

Seven, six, five ...

Four, three, two, one.

Miss Dawn claps for her class!

Published in the United States of America by Cherry Lake Publishing Group
Ann Arbor, Michigan
www.cherrylakepublishing.com

Photo Credits: Cover: © Ilin Sergey/Shutterstock.com; pages 2–11, 13: © Monkey Business Images/
Shutterstock.com; page 12: © Ann in the uk/Shutterstock.com; page 15, Back Cover: © Antonova
Ganna/Shutterstock.com

Cherry Blossom Press is an imprint of Cherry Lake Publishing Group.

Library of Congress Cataloging-in-Publication Data has been filed and is available at catalog.loc.gov.

Cherry Lake Publishing Group would like to acknowledge the work of the Partnership for 21st Century
Learning, a Network of Battelle for Kids. Please visit http://www.battelleforkids.org/networks/p21
for more information.

Printed in the United States of America
Corporate Graphics

Amanda Gebhardt is a curriculum writer and editor and a life-long learner. She lives in Ann Arbor,
Michigan, with her husband, two kids, and one playful pup named Cookie.